Our Earth

Our Earth is a beautiful planet with green and blue patches of land and water on it.

Quick Fact
Earth is called the 'Blue planet' because 70% of its surface is covered with water.

Continents

Continents are the big land masses on Earth. There are seven continents.

Quick Fact
Among all the seven continents, Asia is the largest.

World Map

Mountains

Mountains are the landforms that rise high above the surrounding areas and have sloping sides.

Quick Fact
Some mountains are also present at the bottom of the sea.

Landforms

The formation of land like the mountains, valleys, plateaus, etc. on the surface of the Earth is called landform.

Quick Fact
Glaciers are types of landforms. They are huge masses of ice that flow slowly down the mountains where they are formed.

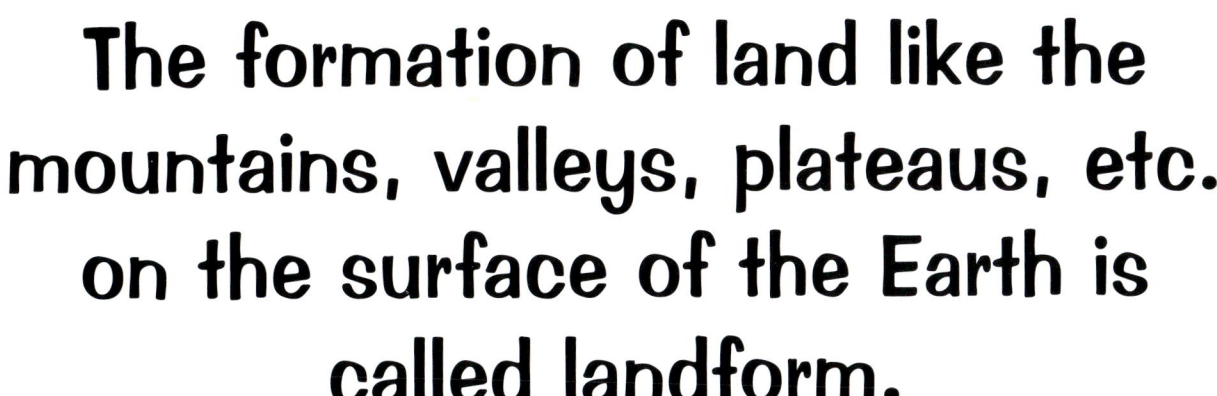

Forest

A forest is a large area of land covered with tall trees, bushes and shrubs. It has various types of animals and birds living in it.

Quick Fact
Cutting down of forests can cause floods, a rise in temperature and the death of many animals and birds.

Oceans, seas and rivers

Oceans, seas and rivers are water bodies on the surface of the Earth.

Quick Fact
The water bodies like oceans, seas and rivers occupy more than half of our planet Earth.

Islands

An island is a piece of land surrounded by water on all sides.

Quick Fact
The world's largest island is Greenland.

Water cycle

Water cycle is the movement of water from the land to the sky and back again to the land.

Quick Fact: The longest river on Earth is the River Nile in Africa.

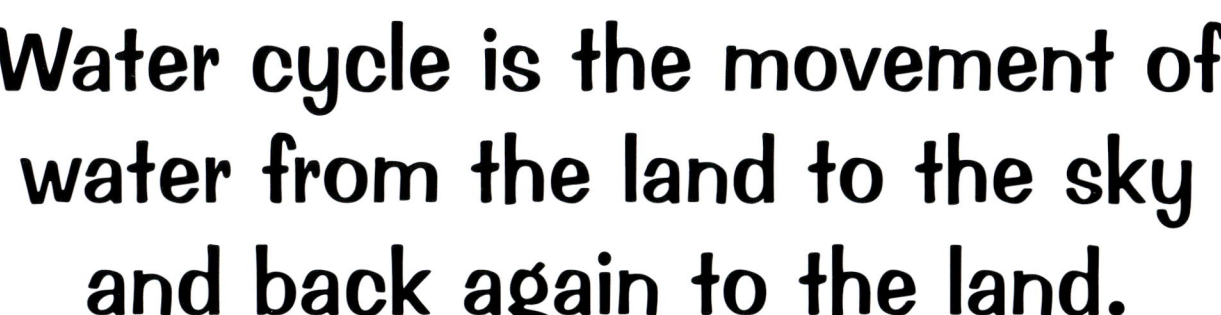

Precious water

Close the tap while you are brushing your teeth.

Quick Fact
Around 95% of a jellyfish is made of water.

Fish

The oceans, seas and rivers are full of fish.

Quick Fact
The largest fish in the world is the whale shark.

Earthquake

The sudden shaking and trembling of the Earth's surface is called an earthquake. During earthquakes, buildings collapse and trees get uprooted.

Quick Fact
The deadliest known earthquake in history took place in China in the year 1556.

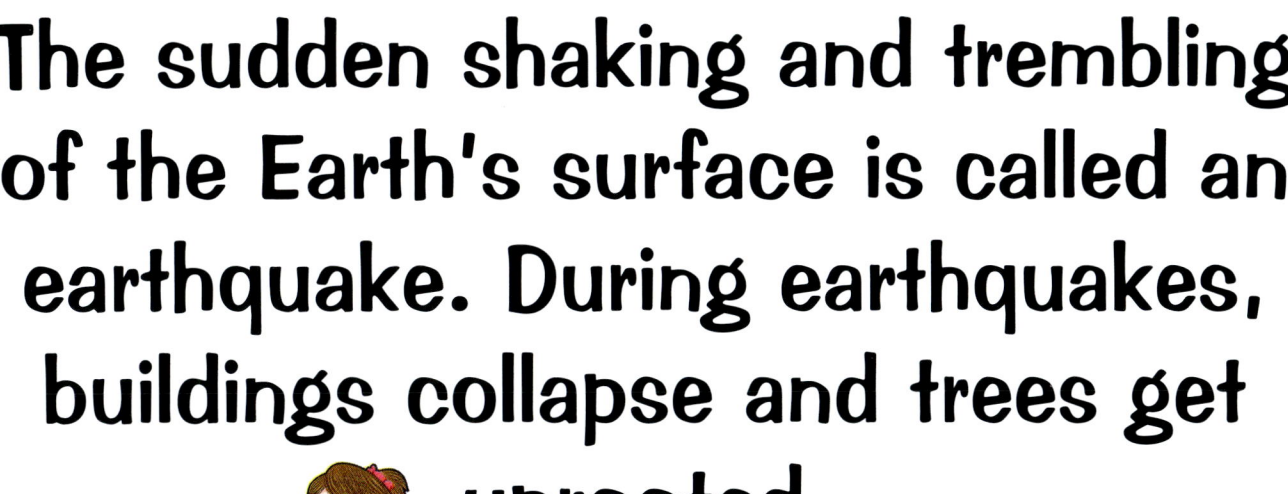

Volcano

Openings on the Earth's surface through which molten rocks, gases, ashes, etc. are thrown out are called volcanoes.

Quick Fact
The largest volcano on Earth is Mauna Loa on Hawaii Island.

Tornado

A tornado is a violent windstorm which comes with a twisting, funnel-shaped cloud.

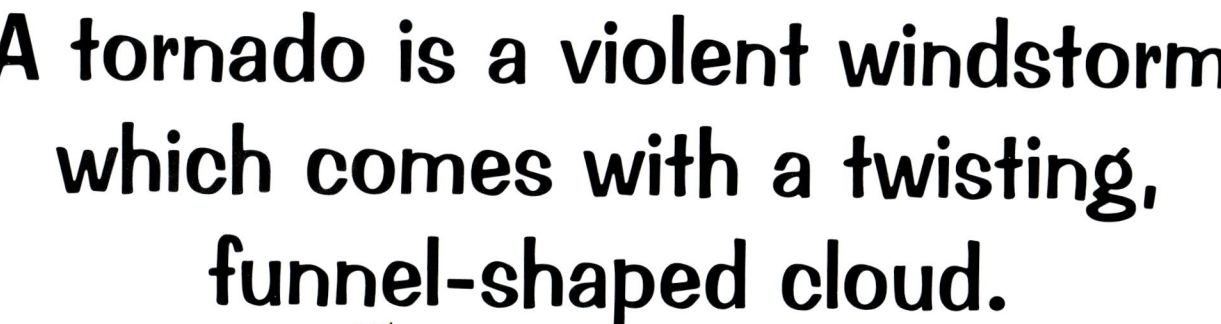

Quick Fact
Did you know that United Kingdom gets about 60 tornadoes a year!